ABSOLUTE BEGINNERS
Keyboard

BOOK TWO

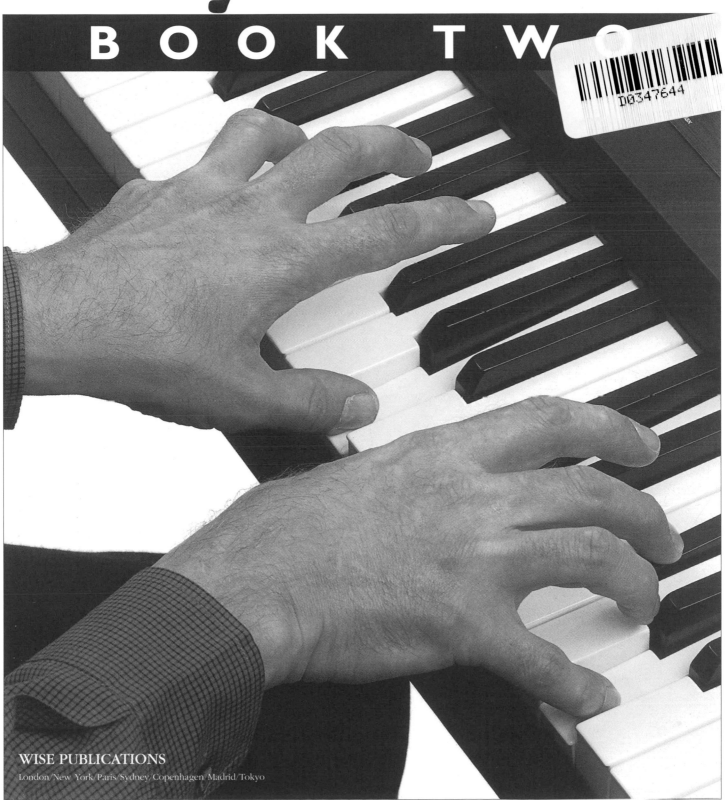

WISE PUBLICATIONS
London/New York/Paris/Sydney/Copenhagen/Madrid/Tokyo

D0347644

Exclusive Distributors:
Music Sales Limited
8/9 Frith Street,
London W1D 3JB, England.

Music Sales Corporation
257 Park Avenue South
New York
NY10010, USA.

Music Sales Pty Limited
120 Rothschild Avenue,
Rosebery, NSW 2018,
Australia.

Order No. AM969694
ISBN 0-7119-8774-2
This book © Copyright 2001 by Wise Publications
www.musicsales.com

Written and arranged by Daniel Scott
Edited by Sorcha Armstrong
Music processed by Paul Ewers and Daniel Scott
Models: Andrew King and Arthur Dick
Keyboard kindly loaned by World Of Pianos
Cover and text photographs by George Taylor
Other photographs courtesy of LFI/Redferns
Book design by Chloë Alexander

Printed in the United Kingdom by Printwise (Haverhill) Limited,
Haverhill, Suffolk.

Your Guarantee of Quality:
As publishers, we strive to produce every book to the highest
commercial standards. This book has been carefully designed to
minimise awkward page turns and to make playing from it a real
pleasure. Particular care has been given to specifying acid-free,
neutral-sized paper made from pulps which have not been
elemental chlorine bleached. This pulp is from farmed sustainable
forests and was produced with special regard for the environment.
Throughout, the printing and binding have been planned to
ensure a sturdy, attractive publication which should give years of
enjoyment. If your copy fails to meet our high standards, please
inform us and we will gladly replace it.

Music Sales' complete catalogue describes thousands of titles
and is available in full colour sections by subject, direct from
Music Sales Limited. Please state your areas of interest and send
a cheque/postal order for £1.50 for postage to:
Music Sales Limited, Newmarket Road, Bury St. Edmunds,
Suffolk IP33 3YB.

Got any comments?
E-mail: absolutebeginners@musicsales.co.uk

www.musicsales.com

Contents

Introduction

Welcome to Absolute Beginners Keyboard Book Two.

In Book One, we looked at the best way to sit at the keyboard, at numbering the fingers of your left and right hand and your ideal hand position.

You learned to
• identify where notes are on the keyboard (white notes anyway!)

You also learned to
• count and play simple rhythms, first with your right hand, then with your left hand, then hands together, using semibreves, minims, crotchets and finally quavers.

Chords were introduced and some movement of notes in one hand against chords in the other hand was tried out – successfully we hope!

Three beats in a bar made a late appearance and the pieces at the end of the book helped to make you feel that your knowledge was leading somewhere in terms of keyboard playing.

In Book Two

There are lots more pieces to play, which should help you to feel extra confidence about some of these exciting new ideas.

The accompanying CD has all of these pieces on it, with both the piano piece demonstrated and a full backing track to play along with, so that you can be the centre of welcome attention!

Don't forget to practise and don't be afraid to go over the same piece a number of times. You are gaining in both strength and confidence when you do this.

At the back of the book you will find further recommendations for other music available for piano and keyboard. We hope that Absolute Beginners Keyboard Book Two will have set you on the path of life-long enjoyment of keyboard playing.

Now let's get started!

Tip

Absolute Beginners Keyboard Book Two will guide you through a number of exciting new things, including

quaver rests • new notes for left and right hand • new chords • scales • keys and key signatures
sharps and flats • 6/8 time signature

Don't forget the ideal
playing position –
as shown here

Don't forget to
keep a straight back.

And your finger numbers
(we can't tell you this enough times!)

Left hand

Right hand

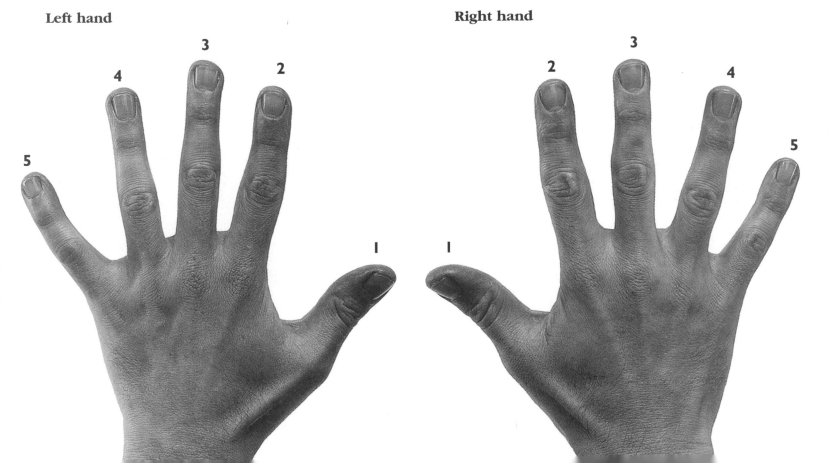

More reminders

Don't forget – your wrist should be in line with the keyboard, not below it.

Imagine that you are holding (not gripping) a tennis ball in each hand, with your hands facing upward. Now turn your hands over and let the imaginary tennis balls go – your hands are in more or less the right position for playing.

And finally a reminder of the keyboard layout:

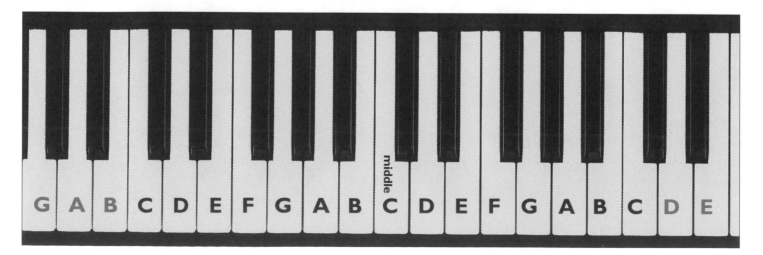

New pieces to play

Let's get playing! We'll start with a famous tune by Beethoven, 'Ode to Joy'. Listen to **Track 1** first – the demonstration track, practise or listen a few times, then have a go yourself with the backing track (**Track 2**).

Track 1
demonstration

Track 2
backing track

Ode To Joy

Traditional

Here's a simple tune from the time of Henry VIII. We've kept the left hand part very simple, so you can concentrate on the slightly more difficult right hand part.

Track 3
demonstration

Track 4
backing track

Stately Dance

repeat from the beginning

Track 5
demonstration   Track 6
backing track

Walking Along

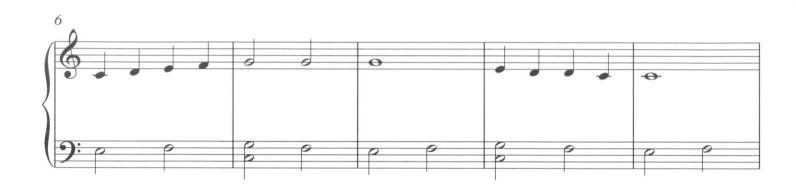

Track 7
demonstration

Track 8
backing track

Let's go back and look at quavers (eighth notes) again. Remember the "tea" and "coffee" sound of their rhythm? A full afternoon tea is now being served:

Tea, cof-fee, tea, cof-fee, bis-cuits, sand-wich-es, tea, cof-fee, tea, cof-fee and some cake.

Tea, cof-fee, tea, cof-fee, bis-cuits, sand-wich-es, tea, cof-fee, tea, cof-fee and more cake!

Track 9
demonstration

Track 10
backing track

Hungry yet? Let's torment ourselves further by playing the same hunger-inducing tune in 3/4 (waltz) time:

Dotted crotchets

Count this rhythm out loud:

| & 2 & 3 & 4 &

Now keep counting but clap only on the notes shown below.
You'll soon find a pattern emerging – this is a basic dotted note rhythm.

A dotted crotchet ♩. lasts for 3 quavers – a dot after a note makes it half as long again.

You could also try clapping continuous quavers but clap louder on the notes that are crossed:

Here's a piece which uses dotted crotchets – in both hands!

Track 11
demonstration

Track 12
backing track

Sombrero

Use second finger

Use third finger

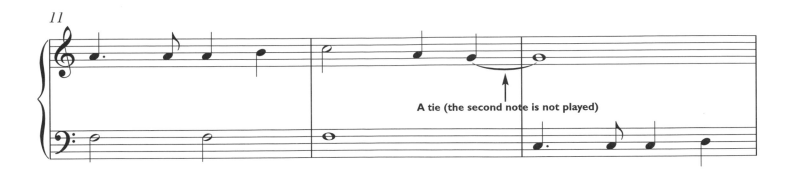

A tie (the second note is not played)

Slower...............

Theme From Symphony No.9

Track 13
demonstration

Track 14
backing track

Here's a tune by Franz Schubert, played "between" the hands (so each hand gets a turn at practising dotted crotchets).

Traditional

Quaver rests

A quaver rest looks like this:

You'll remember from Book One that when you see a rest you should leave a silence instead of playing a note.

Using quaver rests can lead to all sorts of new rhythms. Try (not too fast!) clapping and counting:

Now here's a right-hand melody in the same rhythm that you've just clapped and counted:

Savvy

Track 15
demonstration

Track 16
backing track

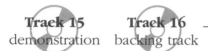

Try playing it again while tapping ♩s with your left hand on your left leg. This should help you with co-ordination and also get you used to playing different rhythms with each hand.

CHECKPOINT

WHAT YOU'VE ACHIEVED SO FAR...

You can now:
- Play eight new pieces
- Play dotted-note rhythms in both hands
- Read and understand quaver rests

Here are some pieces designed to familiarise you with
rests and playing dotted rhythms.

Curious

Track 17
demonstration

Track 18
backing track

Here's another opportunity to practise playing a
melody "between" the hands (sharing the tune!).
Watch out for the left hand finger change at bars 6-7.

Come To The Cookhouse Door

Track 19
demonstration

Track 20
backing track

Some new chords

As you will remember from Book One, a chord is more than one note played at the same time.
This is our first introduction to MINOR chords.

And now a piece using these new chords as well as some of the MAJOR chords you learned in Book One. This is fun to play with the accompaniment on the CD! Note the left hand fingerings – they really help.

Track 21
demonstration

Track 22
backing track

Walking Briskly

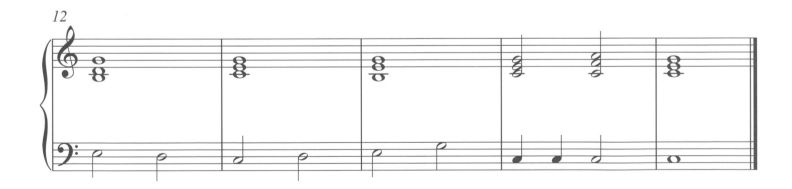

New left hand notes

We now introduce five new left hand notes,
which will help you to play pieces using the
MINOR chords.

B

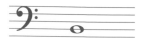

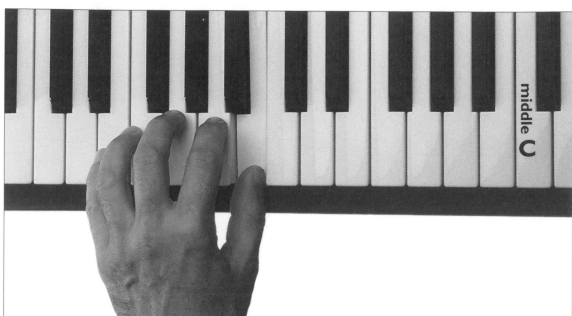

A

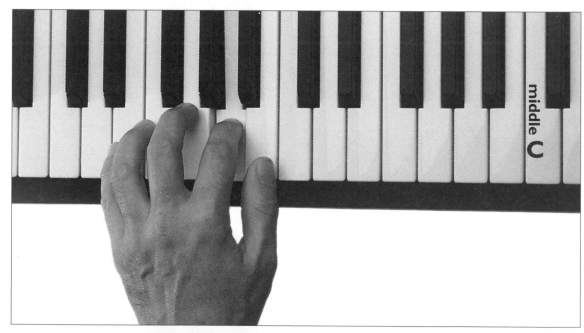

G

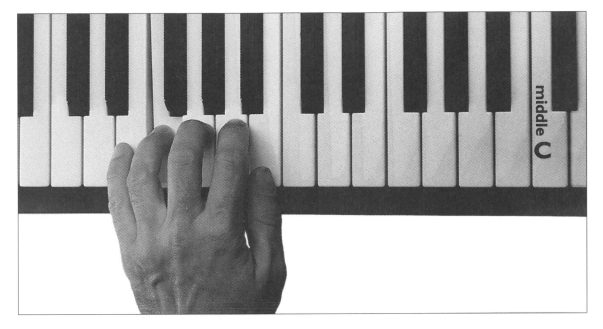

F

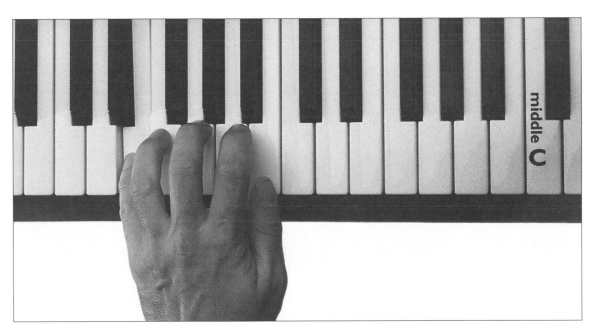

E

Tip

Practise saying out loud the name of each note to make it easier to remember when you start to read it from the score.

More songs

Track 23 demonstration   **Track 24** backing track

Far North

Track 25 demonstration   **Track 26** backing track

In Three

And now here's a Russian piece that makes use
of the new left-hand notes as well as of silences.
Watch out for the change of hand position at bar 10.

Track 27
demonstration

Track 28
backing track

Cossack Dance

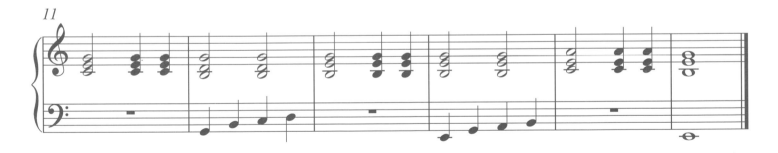

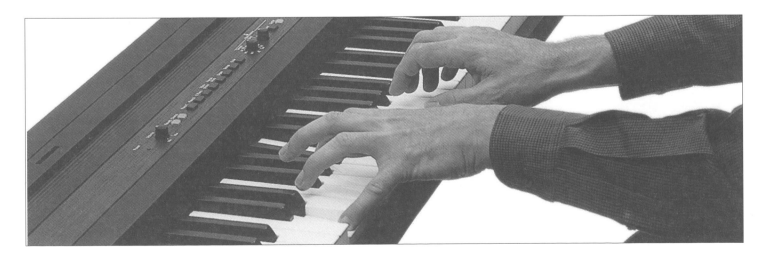

A new time signature 2/4

We've played pieces using 4/4 (4 beats in a bar) and 3/4 (3 beats in a bar). Now let's look a new time signature – 2/4 – which is often used for fairly lively pieces. 2/4 literally means 2 crotchet beats in every bar.

Try counting in 2/4 (it's not very hard!):
1 – 2 /1 – 2 /1 – 2 /1 – 2

We introduced TIES in Book One – in 2/4 time, we can use ties for strong rhythmic effects.

Try clapping this piece first– it's the rhythm of the right hand notes for the piece below.

CHECKPOINT

WHAT YOU'VE ACHIEVED SO FAR...

You have now learnt:
• Three new chords – Am, Dm and Em

• Five new left-hand notes – B, A, G, F and E

• How to count and play in 2/4 time

Track 29
demonstration

Track 30
backing track

Silly Thoughts

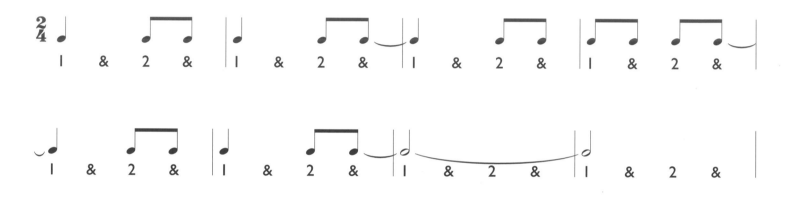

9

Here's another piece in 2/4 to help you
get the feel of this new time-signature.

Horn Calls

Track 31
demonstration

Track 32
backing track

Bear Baiting

Now you're ready to try a slightly longer piece, in ⁴/₄.
This uses the new chords you've learned in the right
hand, and a left-hand melody.

A SCALE is a row of notes, usually starting on one note (C for example) and finishing on the same note. Here is a scale of C (starting and ending on C):

Did you notice that there is no note between E and F or between B and C on the keyboard?

All of the other notes are separated by a black note.

The distance between E and F, and B and C, is called a SEMITONE, but the distance between C and D, for instance, is called a TONE (2 semitones).

So the pattern for a scale of C (and in fact all major scales) is like this:

TONE – TONE – SEMITONE – TONE – TONE – TONE – SEMITONE

Try 'transposing' this tone-semitone pattern to other starting notes – it should still sound like a major scale wherever you start on the keyboard!

When you try and play a scale of C, you will probably find that you "run out" of fingers! So if you start on C with your thumb, you run out on G.

To get around this, you have to smoothly pass your thumb underneath when you get to F.

Tip

This fingering pattern is the basis for many major scales and will also help you when you're playing scale-based melodies in pieces.

Try this scale with the fingerings marked:

pass thumb under

Did you do it smoothly? And now back down again:

pass 3rd finger over

Using the C major scale

Here's a piece which makes use of the scale of C major. You need to follow the fingering, especially when you have to pass your thumb under or a finger over your thumb. Why not fill in the other fingerings yourself?

Track 35
demonstration

Track 36
backing track

Kite Flying

If you see a SHARP (♯) sign in front of a note, it means the note is raised by a SEMITONE.

Here, we're going to look at F♯. Find F on the keyboard, then play the black note directly to the right of F. This is F♯ – it should be between F and G.

If you're still not sure where F♯ is, have a look at the photo on page 27.

Now try the following melody and enjoy the sound of your first F sharp (F♯).

Black And White Rag

Track 37 demonstration   **Track 38** backing track

If a piece has a repeated F sharp in the bar, you don't need to put a ♯ sign in front of the note

DC = go back to the beginning; al FINE play until FINE (end in Italian)

B flat

If you see a FLAT (♭) sign in front of a note, it means the note is lowered by a SEMITONE.

The next piece features B♭. B♭ is the black note between A and B, or just to the left of B. Have a look at the photo opposite if you're not sure.

Now try this piece, being careful to play all the Bs flat – and don't forget the Bs in the left hand!

Track 39
demonstration

Track 40
backing track

Away In A Manger

Traditional

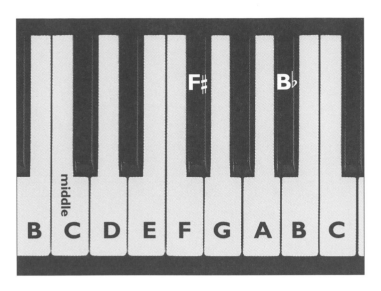

Rather than having to put a sharp or a flat sign in front of a note every time, you can use a KEY SIGNATURE.

This means that every time an F comes up, it becomes F sharp:

Key of G major

Or every time a B comes up, it becomes B flat:

Key of F major

A key means that the strongest note of the scale (C in C major for instance) feels like the "finishing" note of the piece. So a piece is described as being "in C" or "in G" or "in F".

So, next time someone says "Let's play this in G" – you'll know what they mean!

The next 2 pieces are in F major and G major – one piece in each key.

Maryanne

Track 41
demonstration

Track 42
backing track

More songs

Here's a piece in the key of G – don't forget to play every F you see as F sharp – the black note just to the right of F. If you do keep forgetting, why not mark them up on this page (in pencil, as eventually you should be able to read it easily without!).

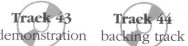

Track 43
demonstration

Track 44
backing track

Semi-circles

Yankee Doodle

Traditional

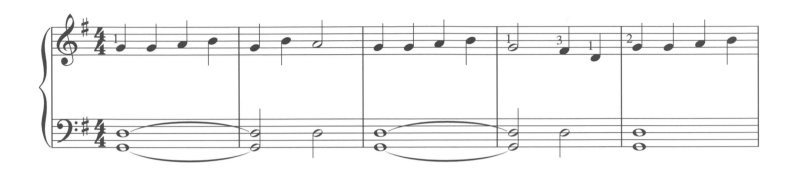

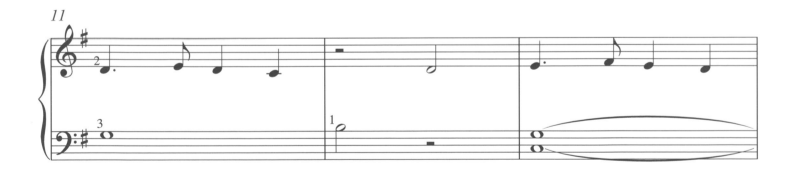

New right hand notes

C

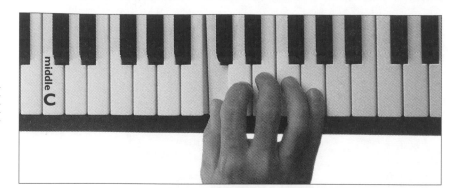

D

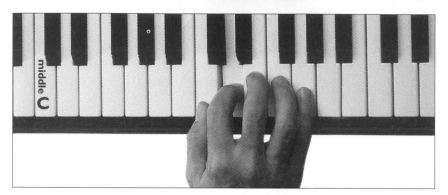

E

F

G

Scales of G major and F major

Now that you know some extra right hand notes you can play two new scales, each with their own KEY SIGNATURE – so don't forget the F sharp in the scale of G major and the B flat in the scale of F major!

Scale of G major

Scale of F major

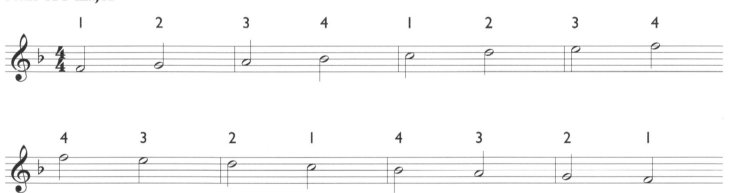

Next, we will play some new pieces in these new keys, using the scales you've just learned as well as lots of other things you've learned.

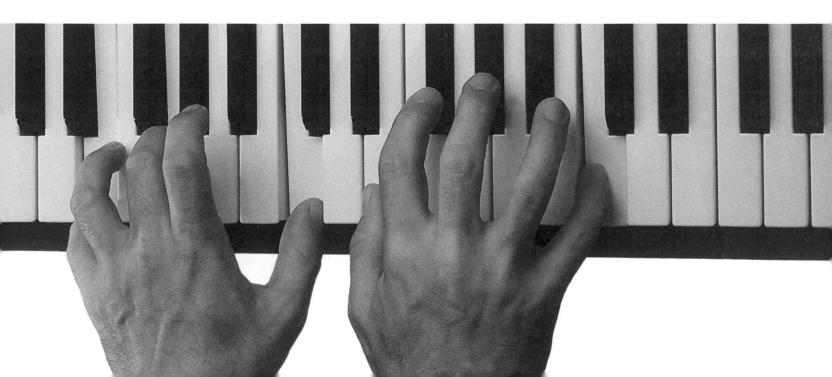

Track 47
demonstration

Track 48
backing track

Nobody Knows

Traditional

A new note D#

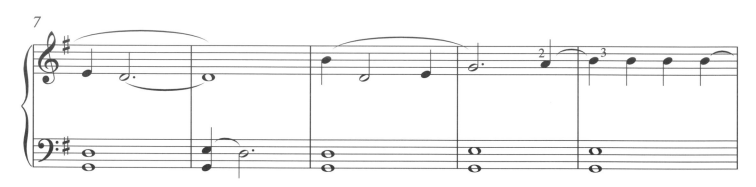

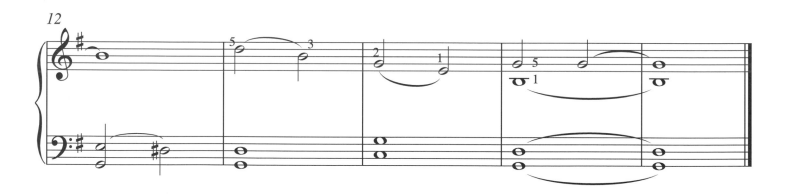

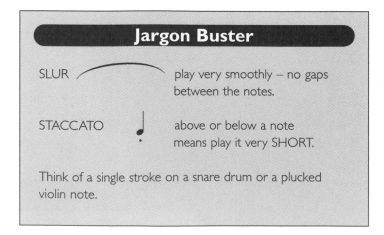

Jargon Buster

SLUR   play very smoothly – no gaps between the notes.

STACCATO   above or below a note means play it very SHORT.

Think of a single stroke on a snare drum or a plucked violin note.

CHECKPOINT
WHAT YOU'VE ACHIEVED SO FAR...

You can now:
- Play the scales of C major, G major and F major
- Understand the concept of key signatures
- Play and read seven new right hand notes: C, D, E, F, F# G and B♭
- Play slurred or staccato

Little Brown Jug

Track 49
demonstration

Track 50
backing track

Traditional

© Copyright 2001 Dorsey Brothers Music Limited, 8/9 Frith Street, London W1.
All Rights Reserved. International Copyright Secured.

Minor keys and scales

The next piece is in E minor. There is one sharp in the key signature, but the note that feels like the "home" note is E rather than G. The TONES and SEMITONES are different in a minor scale:

Track 51
demonstration

Track 52
backing track

Russian Song

Here is the scale of D minor:

The next piece (over the page), which is in D minor, has a number of special features.

First of all, it starts with a quaver upbeat.
If you counted the whole bar, you would say
1 & 2 & 3 & 4 AND and come in on the last AND.

This piece also has some DYNAMICS. These are little symbols that suggest how loudly or softly you should play. These are listed on the right.

Music has lots of these helpful symbols to tell you about aspects of performing that are important. This is sometimes called EXPRESSION.

f

means loud (the Italian word for loud is forte)

p

means soft (the Italian word for soft is piano)

cresc.

means gradually get louder.

>

means accented – play with more force.

When you play 'Peasant Dance', follow the dynamics as well as the slurs, the staccato marks and the fingerings! And of course the notes, but we hope you are feeling quite confident about the notes by now...

There is a new rhythm in this piece. Try clapping and counting it first:

If you prepare well for 'Peasant Dance', it should create an excellent effect!

Peasant Dance

$^6/_8$ means there are six quavers in every bar – 1-2-3-4-5-6, 1-2-3-4-5-6.

Usually, but not always, they are divided into two groups of three – 1-2-3 4-5-6, 1-2-3 4-5-6

You might be thinking that $^3/_4$ time also has six quavers in a bar. The difference is that $^3/_4$ time is thought of as being three crotchets in a bar instead of six quavers, and is usually counted like this: 1-2 3-4 5-6.

The next piece, in E minor, is in $^6/_8$. This piece introduces:

mf   which means moderately loud (Italian words mezzo forte)

mp   which means moderately soft (Italian words mezzo piano)

and

dim.   or   ———————

which means get quieter gradually.

Tip

What's the point of time signatures?

They define the main beat of the music.

Every time you tap your foot to a piece of music, you're actually responding to the time signature.

Follow My Lead

Track 55
demonstration

Track 56
backing track

Another piece in D minor

Here's a reminder of ties, dotted crotchets and quaver rests.

Track 57
demonstration   **Track 58**
backing track

Questing

In a relatively short space of time, you have covered a lot of ground and learned over 30 new pieces!

You should be ready to play a whole world of piano and keyboard music – some classic piano pieces are listed on the right.

Keep practising and don't let your enthusiasm for music and playing die away – it's a wonderful life-long skill that will bring you much pleasure.

Für Elise Beethoven

She's the One Robbie Williams

Lady Madonna The Beatles

Clair de Lune Debussy

Imagine John Lennon

Minuet in G Bach

Gymnopedie no 1 Satie

Waltz in A flat Brahms

Trouble Coldplay

Lucille Little Richard

The Beatles

Little Richard

CHECKPOINT

WHAT YOU'VE ACHIEVED SO FAR...

You've learnt how to:

- Recognise and use dynamics such as forte, piano and crescendo

- Play the scales of E minor and D minor

- Count a new time signature – 6/8

Further reading

Now you're ready to move onto more advanced material. There's a wealth of music of different styles out there for you to enjoy, but why not investigate some of the titles below; they'll help you continue to develop your technique, and will introduce you to some of the great keyboard repertoire that you'll be able to play. See the Music Sales Catalogue for the full list of titles (details on page 2).

The Complete Keyboard Player Series

The most comprehensive series of books for piano and keyboard available, with 50+ titles. Each book contains a collection of pieces by artists such as Abba, The Beatles, and Gershwin, or styles such as Jazz, Blues, Pops, and Film and TV Themes, The series is supplemented by 9 specially-arranged songbooks and there are also four tutor books available.

The Complete Keyboard Player Book 1 (Tutor Book)
Contains 15 famous songs including 'Let It Be', 'Super Trouper' and 'Blowin' In The Wind'. Instrumental backing track includes piano, guitar, percussion and many others.
AM91383

The Complete Keyboard Player Abba
Sixteen classic Abba songs arranged for keyboard. Includes 'Thank You For The Music', 'Mamma Mia', and 'Dancing Queen'.
AM91095

The Complete Keyboard Player Movie Music
A superb collection of film music from the big screen. Includes 'Schindler's List', 'Circle of Life', 'Love is All Around' and 'Goldeneye'.
AM938234

FastForward

An exciting new series of instrumental instruction books. Includes hints and tips with easy-to-follow instructions and advice. The accompanying CD allows you to listen and then play along with the specially-recorded backing tracks.

FastForward: Cool Blues Keyboard
Superb book and CD pack, with help on learning riffs, octave rundowns, and turnarounds, to help you get that genuine blues feel on your keyboard.
AM934835

FastForward: Dynamic Rock Keyboards
Learn to play full, rich dynamic piano riffs and fills, swirling organ sounds and effects, moody electric piano chords and much more with this exciting book and CD pack.
AM92437

Fastforward: Boogie Woogie Piano
Learn to play authentic left-hand rhythmic patterns, sparkling riffs, and discover the secrets of syncopation, arpeggios, grace notes, and other essential boogie techniques.
AM958925

Fastforward: Rock'n'Roll Piano
All techniques are explained from basics to advanced techniques, to show you how to become a foot-stomping Rock 'n' Roll player par excellence! Play in the style of Rock 'n' Roll legends such as Little Richard, Ray Charles, Fats Domino and Jerry Lee Lewis.
AM963700